Bath's Railways
in photographs by J. C. Way
Neil Butters

BR standard Class 9F 2-10-0 No. 92220 *Evening Star* on the 8th September 1962, with the last Down Pines Express to run over Somerset & Dorset metals, leaving Bath and about to enter Devonshire Tunnel *en route* to Bournemouth West. The locomotive was the last steam engine to have been built by British Railways, at Swindon Works and is now preserved, at the National Railway Museum in York. Note the train reporting number '1O95' signifying a Class 1 train heading for the Southern Region: 'O'.

BR Standard Class 4 4-6-0 No. 75073 heads out of Bath with the 9.55 am from Bath Green Park to
Templecombe. Taken at the rear of Egerton Road, Bank Holiday Monday 18th May 1959. Note the local
S&D passenger train lamp code: top plus bottom right, looking at locomotive.

© Neil Butters, 2016
First published in the United Kingdom, 2016,
by Stenlake Publishing Ltd.
www.stenlake.co.uk
ISBN 9781840337419

The publishers regret that they cannot supply
copies of any pictures featured in this book.

Printed by:
Berforts, 17 Burgess Road, Hastings, TN35 4NR

Foreword

Our father's combined love of steam trains and photography began in the 1920s when, as a young boy growing up in Penzance, he and his brother would run to the end of their road, sit on the wall overlooking Penzance Station and record the trains that came and went using their Box Brownie camera.

As a young man our father's interests deepened. He acquired a more sophisticated camera and began developing his own black and white photographs, the subject of which was invariably trains.

Later we, as young children, would often be with him at the side of the tracks 'helping' to take the pictures and then we would 'help' him develop and print them with great anticipation of the results. The seeds of our own love of steam trains, and railways in general, were sown.

When our father's employers moved him to Bath in 1958 it was no surprise that he chose a house which had the Somerset and Dorset Railway running in a cutting at the bottom of the garden. We have fond memories of standing on the fence waving to the trains that chugged up the hill from Green Park Station before they disappeared in a cloud of smoke into Devonshire Tunnel. However, the rumble and whoosh of those emerging from the tunnel gave little warning of their approach. We had to be quick to see those.

Our father rented a piece of land from the railway authorities. It was the flat part at the top of the cutting just outside our garden fence. Here he was in his element working the land to produce extra vegetables whilst trains went up and down the line, his camera often to hand.

Through his hobbies he inadvertently recorded a small slice of history, as portrayed in this book for although the Great Western main line still very much continued, albeit without steam, the Somerset and Dorset line closed in March 1966. However, many felt that the line had lost its soul in 1962 when the famous Pines Express was diverted to run via Reading. We remember it clearly. The day was tinged with sadness as we watched the last train make its way along the line, but thankfully Dad was there to record it.

Jan Walker, Anne Pickard and Susan Way

This book is dedicated to the memory of our mother, Pam, much loved wife of John Corin Way.

J. C. Way, photographer.

Introduction

Isambard Kingdom Brunel famously brought his Great Western Railway (GWR) here first, what is now Bath Spa Station ('Spa' was added in 1949) opening on 31st August 1840. This was laid to broad gauge, the rails being seven feet and a quarter of an inch apart, as distinct from the standard four feet eight and a half inches.

The last broad gauge train ran on 20th May 1892, with the rails altered – remarkably – over one weekend all the way from London to Penzance.

Twerton-on-Avon (originally just Twerton – closed 1917), Saltford (closed 1970 – but possibly to be reopened), and Keynsham (known between 1925 and 1974 as Keynsham and Somerdale) all opened in 1840.

Bath's original service ran to and from Bristol (Temple Meads) only. The line east through Box Tunnel – then the longest railway tunnel in the world, which took a full five years to construct – was not opened until 1841.

Until the tunnel was completed, a carriage service operated over Box Hill. Indeed, due to scare stories about what might happen to people travelling at speed in such a long tunnel, the carriage service continued for a while even after the line was fully open!

Next on the scene in Bath itself was the Midland Railway, again from Bristol (Temple Meads) – but also from the north, via a triangular junction at Mangotsfield.

The station – near Queen Square – opened on 4th August 1869. This was formally named Bath (Green Park) on 18th June 1951.

Other stations on the line, from 1869, in the district were at Weston (closed 1953), and Kelston for Saltford (closed 1949) – the latter built with no road access!

Last to arrive was the Somerset & Dorset Railway (S&D).

This also ran into the Midland station, from 1874, producing a north-south route, connecting for example Manchester with Bournemouth. Unfortunately, it went into receivership the following year and became jointly owned by the Midland Railway and the London & South Western Railway – whereupon it was renamed the Somerset & Dorset Joint Railway. Following the 1923 Grouping, ownership passed to the London Midland & Scottish Railway and the Southern Railway.

The most famous train on the line was the *Pines Express*, which ran as such between 1927 and 1962 before diversion away via Reading.

Both lines into Green Park Station were closed as of 7th March 1966 – albeit the station itself remains, and indeed in fine shape.

Other lines that ran through the district were the Trowbridge Branch of the GWR – still very much open, the Bristol & North Somerset, and the Camerton Branch. This last was made famous by the filming of the *Titfield Thunderbolt*, especially, in 1952.

Stations and locations that feature in the photographs that follow include: Bath Spa, Oldfield Park, Twerton, Box Tunnel (GWR); and Bath (Green Park), Devonshire Tunnel, Lyncombe Vale, and Midford (S&D).

The most famous features on the northern section of the Somerset & Dorset were Devonshire and Combe Down Tunnels, Tucking Mill and Midford Viaducts, and Midford Station platform, all now easily seen from the superb Two Tunnels cycle and footpath – opened 6th April 2013.

Bath has a rich railway history. It was therefore a delightful surprise to come across the steam-era photographic collection in print form of the late J.C. Way, still held locally by his three daughters who have generously allowed its reproduction coincident with the 50th anniversary of the commemoration of the closure of the Somerset & Dorset line in March 1966. Enjoy them!

LMS 2P 4-4-0 No. 40601 pilots BR Standard 5MT 4-6-0 No. 73017 as they pass the Moorlands Estate on the approach to Bath Green Park on the Somerset & Dorset Joint Line, July 1958.

Castle Class No. 4091 *Dudley Castle* with a Down Paddington – Plymouth express (6.45 pm from Bath Spa), approaching Oldfield Park Station, 30th August 1958.

King Class 4-6-0 No. 6023 *King Edward II* with the Down Merchant Venturer: 1.05 pm from Bath Spa, 1st November 1958. Locomotive now preserved.

In May 1959 LMS 2P 4-4-0 No. 40564 pilots an unknown BR Standard loco on the Down Pines Express in the cutting behind Egerton Road, Bath. The train is about to enter Devonshire Tunnel.

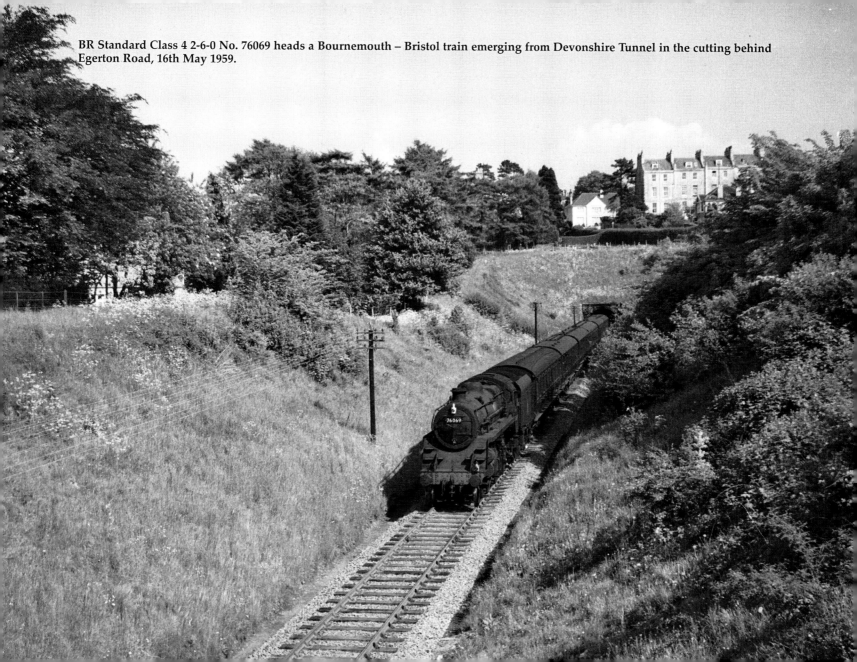

BR Standard Class 4 2-6-0 No. 76069 heads a Bournemouth – Bristol train emerging from Devonshire Tunnel in the cutting behind Egerton Road, 16th May 1959.

Castle Class No. 5066 *Sir Felix Pole* with the Down Merchant Venturer leaving Bath Spa at 1.05 pm on 16th May 1959. Sir Felix was General Manager of the GWR (1921–1929). The locomotive was originally named *Wardour Castle* and received its new name in April 1956, following his death in January of that year. The name continued for some years on Class 43 High Speed Train locomotive No. 43131 which was named *Sir Felix Pole* on 23rd August 1985.

BR Standard Class 4 4-6-0 No. 75073 heads out of Bath with the 9.55 am from Bath Green Park to Bournemouth. Taken at the rear of Cotswold Road, 18th May 1959.

No. 6028 *King George VI* with the Down 3.23 pm from Bath Spa (Paddington – Weston-super-Mare train) passing Oldfield Park, Sunday 7th June 1959.

Class 4300 2-6-0s Nos. 6391 and 5384 light engines at Oldfield Park, 20th June 1959.

The first of the modern era: Warship Class Type 4 B-B diesel hydraulic No. D806 *Cambrian* with the 4.15 pm Paddington to Plymouth train entering Bath Spa Station to depart at 6.30 pm, 8th July 1959.

No. 1019 *County of Merioneth* and No. 5027 *Farleigh Castle* double heading with the 12.30 pm Paddington – Weston-super-Mare train, between Bathampton and Bath, 12th July 1959.

Class 2P No. 40569 with West Country No. 34028 *Eddystone* leaving Bath on the 2.10 pm from Green Park with the Saturdays Only Nottingham – Bournemouth West train, 15th August 1959.

No. 2251 Class 3MT 0-6-0 No. 2265 with a Down goods emerging from the western portal of Box Tunnel, 15th August 1959.

Castle Class No. 5073 *Blenheim* with a Down train emerging from the western portal of Twerton Tunnel, 22nd August 1959.

No. 5000 *Launceston Castle* at Twerton Tunnel Signal Box with the 1.18 pm Saturdays Only Paddington – Weston-super-Mare train departing Bath Spa 4.03 pm, 22nd August 1959. Note the impressive telegraph poles and wires.

BR Standard Class 5 4-6-0 No. 73019 leaves Devonshire Tunnel at Lyncombe Vale with the 9.30 am Sundays Bristol–Bournemouth train, 30th August 1959.

S&D 7F 2-8-0 No. 53806 (S&D 4F 0-6-0 No. 44561 at rear) on a Down goods passing the rear of Egerton Road. It was one of eleven designed by Henry Fowler specifically for the S&D. Wednesday 14th October 1959.

No. 6019 *King Henry V* with the 12.30 pm (Sundays) from Paddington – Weston-super-Mare, between Bathampton and Bath. Taken from the canal bank, 31st January 1960.

No. 5008 *Raglan Castle* with the 12.30 pm (Sundays) from Paddington – Weston-super-Mare (3.23 pm from Bath Spa), passing Oldfield Park, 21st February 1960.

BR Standard Class 5 No. 73028 with the 1.10 pm Green Park to Templecombe. Taken in cutting at bottom of garden, Egerton Road. The small oval at the bottom of the smokebox door is the shed code; 82F was Bath Green Park. The 'SC' below that means that the locomotive had a self-cleaning smokebox. Saturday 5th March 1960.

B-B Warship No. D811 *Daring* with the 4.15 pm Paddington – Plymouth (6.30 from Bath Spa), approaching Oldfield Park Station, 12th May 1960.

BR Standard Class 4 4-6-0 No. 75072 with the 1.10 pm Green Park to Templecombe. Taken near the Co-op Bakery, 14th May 1960.

S&D 4F 0-6-0 No. 44557 at Midford (dep 3.31 pm) with the 3.20 pm from Bath Green Park – Templecombe. The locomotive carries the shed code 82G: Templecombe. 14th May 1960.

Warship No. D801 *Vanguard* with the 4.15 pm Paddington – Plymouth express (6.30 from Bath Spa). Approaching Oldfield Park, 14th May 1960.

BR Standard Class 9F 2-10-0 No. 92237 with an Up freight passing Oldfield Park Station. 7.45 am, 24th May 1960.

28th May 1960. No. 7024 *Powis Castle* **with the 1.40 pm Paddington – Weston-super-Mare (dep Bath Spa 4.03 pm), between Oldfield Park and Twerton, passing former S&D bridge recently demolished as part of the electrification works, but to be replaced with a new cycle and footbridge.**

No. 5040 *Stokesay Castle* near Beckford Gardens. Bath with the 12.30 pm Paddington – Weston-super-Mare (Sundays) train (dep Bath Spa 3.23 pm). Note the flat-sided tender. 6th June 1960.

On the 7th June 1960, BR Standard Class 3 2-6-2 Tank No. 82009, with a B set of coaches, arriving at the Up platform of Bath Spa with the 7.52 am Bath Spa – Westbury. The train is passing Bath Corporation's Generating Station in Dorchester Street, which closed in 1966 and was demolished the following year.

No. 1011 *County of Chester* at Bath Spa with an 8.00 am special to Paddington, 7th June 1960.

No. 6025 *King Henry III* (with the BR Western Region head code 007!) arriving at the Up platform, Bath Spa with the 7.00 am Weston-super-Mare to Paddington (8.05 am from Bath), 7th June 1960.

Class 9F No. 92204 near Maple Grove Bridge heading the 10.05 am Sunday train Green Park to Bournemouth, 21st August 1960.

Hall Class locomotive No. 5949, *Trematon Hall,* with the 10.55 am Bristol Temple Meads to Portsmouth approaches Twerton Tunnel Signal Box, 5th November 1960.

Class 4700 7F 2-8-0 No. 4707 approaches Twerton Tunnel Signal Box with an Up goods. Note the cattle wagon and sheeted china clay wagons. 5th November 1960.

LMS Class 5 4-6-0 No. 45006 with the Up Pines Express leaving Bath Green Park. Taken near Twerton Fork, 5th November 1960.

No. 4085 *Berkeley Castle* with a Down train passing Bathampton, 4 pm, 13th May 1961.

Class 9F No. 92001 entering Combe Down Tunnel with the 10.05 am (Sundays Only) Bath Green Park to Bournemouth West, 23rd July 1961.

BR Standard Class 4 No. 75023 (plus Class 5 No. 73023?) approaching Midford from Bath with the Pines Express, 30th September 1961.

Class 2251 No. 3215 approaches Midford from Bath with the 3.20 pm Bath Green Park – Templecombe. It was rare to see this class of engine on the S&D main line, albeit more common on the branch between Evercreech and Highbridge. 30th September 1961.

No. 4992 *Crosby Hall* with the Ian Allan railtour Western Sunset leaving Bath and passing Bath Junction (near the gasworks and S&D yard), 22nd September 1962.

BR Standard Class 5 No. 73054 with the 9.53 am Green Park to Bournemouth West passing through Lyncombe Vale, 8th June 1963.

SR U Class 4P3F 2-6-0 No. 31639 and West Country No. 34015 *Exmouth* approaching Devonshire Tunnel from Green Park, 2nd January 1966. These locos will have worked on a special. The U Class were trialled on the S&D for regular running, but were not successful.

West Country No. 34006 *Bude* and BR Standard Class 4 Tank No. 80043 at Green Park sheds. The occasion was the Locomotive Club of Great Britain (LCGB) special on the last day of public service on the Somerset & Dorset line, 5th March 1966.

An unidentified High Speed Train (InterCity 125) on the 14.05 Paddington – Bristol at Sydney Gardens, Bath, 15th August 1984. A commonplace scene, apart from the livery, for the moment – but soon there will be overhead wires and new Hitachi trains…

Lowering the embankment that carried the Somerset & Dorset Joint Line over Monksdale Road before the bridge was demolished. This photograph dates from 17th September 1972.